HOME COOKING

First published in Great Britain by Simon & Schuster UK Ltd, 2003
A Viacom Company

Simon & Schuster UK Ltd
Africa House
64–78 Kingsway
London
WC2B 6AH

1 3 5 7 9 10 8 6 4 2

Design: **Fiona Andreanelli**
Typesetting: **Stylize Digital Artwork**
Food photography: **Steve Baxter**
Home economist: **Joss Herd**
Stylist for food photography: **Liz Belton**
Editor: **Deborah Savage**
Printed and bound in China

ISBN 0 74324 013 8

Best-kept Secrets of the Women's Institute

HOME COOKING

Jill Brand and Carrie O'Regan

SIMON & SCHUSTER

A VIACOM COMPANY

CONTENTS

INTRODUCTION

Do you remember the days when families used to sit round the table at mealtimes and enjoy home-cooked food? Nowadays the trend seems to be for eating ready-meals on a tray in front of the TV. But for the tastiest meals, with the freshest ingredients and the best flavours you really can't beat home cooking. And family mealtimes aren't just about food either, a meal should be a chance for the whole family to sit down, relax and chat and eat together.

These days it would be so easy to rely on convenience foods, takeaways and ready-meals but these options are expensive, often tasteless and of poor nutritional value. So what is the solution if you're short on time, but want to enjoy home cooked food? Well, with careful planning and a little help from this book you can prepare tasty fresh meals without spending hours in the kitchen.

The key to good cooking is good ingredients, so start with the basics and when you go shopping look for lean cuts of meat, organic produce from farmers' markets or farm shops, seasonal fruit and vegetables and free-range eggs and opt for locally produced ingredients where possible. Once you've got the best ingredients you can afford, then simply choose your recipe and start cooking.

This book features a wide variety of recipes, from fast suppers that are ideal to enjoy during the week to simple weekend lunches for family and friends. And from hassle-free entertaining where you can relax too, to easy classics that'll you'll love. But whatever the occasion all the recipes in this book are simple, nutritious and delicious – so forget ready-meals next time you go to the supermarket and get back to home cooking!

Each recipe here gives a freezing recommendation. It certainly saves time and effort, in the long run, if you make double quantities of a recipe to freeze. You will then have a meal ready in the time it takes to defrost and reheat the dish, ideal for those days when the whole family arrive home late.

GUIDE TO SUCCESSFUL FREEZING

If your freezer is fitted with a fast freeze switch then better results will be obtained when placing food in the freezer, as smaller particles of ice are formed within the food and the food freezes faster in the colder temperatures. Turn the fast freeze switch on as recommended in your freezer instruction book. Always select containers suitable for the quantity of food, remember that liquids expand on freezing so allow a space above the food in a container, this will ensure that lids are not pushed off from the expanding liquids.

To avoid losing texture and flavour do not freeze any of the foods in this book for more than six weeks, it's easy to ensure this by clearly labelling everything. Pack food in suitable containers so they do not spoil on freezing. Suitable packaging materials include polythene bags which if using for soups can be placed in a rigid container so that when the contents are frozen the package can be stacked in the freezer. Foil dishes are ideal for stews, casseroles and pies; these can then be used in the oven for reheating. Foil containers are not recommended for the microwave.

Foods should be thawed slowly preferably overnight in the refrigerator and then reheated. Always ensure that the food is piping hot throughout before serving.

STORE CUPBOARD INGREDIENTS

Stock up your cupboard, fridge and freezer with some basic foodstuffs and you will never be short of the ingredients for making a wholesome and delicious meal. Today, the home cook can draw upon a range of foods from all over the world, that have a long shelf life and are relatively inexpensive.

IN THE CUPBOARD

Alongside your pepper and salt mill, it is wise to have a variety of dried herbs. Although fresh herbs are usually preferable, some, such as dried oregano, can be more flavourful. Try to have bay leaves, sage and thyme as well. Certain spices and flavourings will certainly stand you in good stead; these are saffron, cumin, coriander, cardamoms, turmeric, cinnamon, nutmeg and vanilla pods. Some good olive oil is an essential for your cupboard as well as sunflower oil. Wine or cider vinegar is invaluable for salad dressings and soy sauce will enhance any stir-fries or oriental-style dishes. If you have cans of tuna and tomatoes, dried pulses, jars of sun-dried tomatoes, olives and capers alongside some dried pasta, rice (risotto as well as long-grain), couscous and polenta you have the makings of a delicious meal without having to step into a shop.

IN THE FRIDGE

Why not have some Parmesan cheese or even some mozzarella to sit alongside the Cheddar in the fridge? Free-range eggs, some good bacon, yogurt and crème fraîche with some unsalted butter can form the makings of a delicious omelette, a Quiche Lorraine, macaroni cheese or pancakes.

Some of the most delicious soups are made from the simplest ingredients and with the addition of a few choice herbs or spices it's so easy to make a tasty and nutritious meal. A bowl of soup often justs hits the spot, whether you want a hearty main course or a light lunch.

Main course salads are increasingly popular and if you're in

SIMPLE SOUPS & SALADS

the mood for something quick and easy for supper then look no further. Arrange in a large bowl or platter and let everyone help themselves. When you're shopping remember that fresh, seasonal ingredients such as crisp leaves, tender beetroot and sweet tomatoes are the key to some of the best, and simplest salads. All the salads in this chapter can also be served as an accompaniment to a main dish or as part of a buffet.

SERVES 4
PREPARATION TIME: 15 minutes
COOKING TIME: 20 minutes
FREEZING: not recommended

The freshly cooked hot potatoes and chicken slightly wilt the leaves in this main course salad, while the zesty lime and balsamic dressing give it a real zing. Serve straight away, with crusty white bread to mop up the juices.

HOT POTATO & CHICKEN SALAD

450 g (1 lb) potatoes, diced
4 boneless, skinless chicken breasts
2 tablespoons sunflower oil
2 tablespoons sesame seeds
225 g (8 oz) salad leaves
10 cherry tomatoes, halved

FOR THE DRESSING:
4 tablespoons olive oil
2 tablespoons balsamic vinegar
zest and juice of 1 lime
salt and freshly ground black pepper

1 Place the potatoes in a pan of salted water and bring to the boil. Reduce the heat to a simmer, cover the pan and cook for 15 minutes until the potatoes are tender. Drain.

2 Slice the chicken breasts into strips. Heat the sunflower oil in a frying pan, add the chicken strips for 4-5 minutes or until cooked. Place on kitchen paper to drain.

3 In a small pan carefully dry fry the sesame seeds until just coloured, take care not to burn them.

4 Whisk together the dressing ingredients in a small jug.

5 Place the salad leaves and tomatoes in a serving bowl. Add the potatoes, chicken and sesame seeds and pour over the dressing, toss all the ingredients together to mix completely. Serve immediately.

SERVES 4–6
PREPARATION TIME: 20 minutes
COOKING TIME: 1 hour
FREEZING: recommended

Roasting the pumpkin first develops its naturally sweet flavour. This is a **wonderfully satisfying** autumnal soup that can be served with granary bread as a warming supper or lunch.

1.8 kg (4 lb) pumpkin, unpeeled,
quartered and de-seeded
4 tablespoons sunflower oil
1 teaspoon ground nutmeg, plus extra
for seasoning
2 medium onions, sliced
700 ml (1¼ pints) vegetable stock
425–575 ml (¾–1 pint) milk
salt and freshly ground black pepper

1 Place the prepared pumpkin on a roasting tray, brush with half the sunflower oil and sprinkle with the nutmeg. Roast at Gas Mark 6/electric oven 200°C/fan oven 180°C for 30–40 minutes until soft.
2 Remove the pumpkin from the oven and carefully peel the skin away from the flesh. Dice the flesh.
3 In a large pan gently cook the onions in the remaining sunflower oil until soft but not coloured, stir in the stock and the pumpkin and cook for 15 minutes.
4 Allow the soup to cool for a few minutes and then liquidise until smooth or push through a fine sieve.
5 Return the soup to a clean pan and stir in enough milk until the desired consistency is reached. Reheat gently, season to taste and add a little extra nutmeg if necessary.

ROASTED PUMPKIN SOUP

SERVES 4–6
PREPARATION TIME: 20 minutes
COOKING TIME: 50 minutes
FREEZING: recommended

A real winter warmer! Spicy sausage adds a robust flavour to this filling soup. Serve with warmed granary rolls or hot garlic bread.

SPICY SAUSAGE SOUP

2 tablespoons sunflower oil
2 garlic cloves, crushed
1 medium onion, chopped
375 g (13 oz) white cabbage, shredded finely
115 g (4 oz) red lentils
400 g can of chopped tomatoes
1 teaspoon dried mixed herbs
575 ml (1 pint) vegetable stock
225 g (8 oz) spicy sausage, chopped
(e.g. chorizo)
salt and freshly ground black pepper

1 In a large pan heat the oil and cook the garlic and onion gently until soft.
2 Stir in the cabbage and fry for 5 minutes.
3 Add the lentils, tomatoes, herbs, stock and seasoning and bring to the boil and simmer for 40 minutes.
4 Adjust the seasoning to taste. Stir in the chopped sausage and heat through for 10 minutes.

A wide variety of ready-to-eat spicy sausages are available from most major supermarkets – try Spanish chorizo, Polish kabanos or Italian pepperoni to add a kick to this simple salad. It is ideal to serve as an accompaniment to a main course or as part of a buffet when you are entertaining.

SERVES 4–6
PREPARATION TIME: 20 minutes
COOKING TIME: 20–25 minutes
FREEZING: not recommended

SPICY SAUSAGE RICE SALAD

175 g (6 oz) long grain brown rice
50 g (2 oz) wild rice
I yellow pepper, de-seeded and diced coarsely
115 g (4 oz) raisins
50 g (2 oz) walnuts, chopped
50 g (2 oz) green olives, pitted
I orange, cut into segments
225 g (8 oz) spicy sausage, chopped
salt and freshly ground black pepper

1 Place the rice in a pan, cover with cold water and bring to the boil. Reduce the heat to a simmer, cover and cook for 20–25 minutes until tender. Drain well, rinse in cold water and allow to cool completely.
2 Place the cooled rice in a large serving bowl. Stir in the remaining ingredients and mix thoroughly.
3 Serve as part of a main course or on a buffet table.

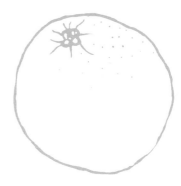

SERVES 4
PREPARATION TIME: 15 minutes
COOKING TIME: 30 minutes
FREEZING: recommended

CELERY & PEANUT SOUP

The **unusual combination** of celery and peanuts works really well in this light vegetarian soup. Serve sprinkled with crumbled Cheshire or Wensleydale cheese and a few chopped fresh chives.

1 In a large pan melt the butter and cook the onion until soft.
2 Add the potato and cook for 5 minutes. Stir in the celery and cook for a further 5 minutes.
3 Stir in the stock, season and bring to the boil, simmer for 15 minutes.
4 Add the milk and peanuts to the pan.
5 Allow the soup to cool slightly and then liquidise until smooth.
6 Return the soup to a clean pan. Reheat gently, season to taste and serve piping hot.

25 g (1 oz) butter
1 medium onion, chopped finely
1 medium potato, diced
4 celery sticks, chopped
575 ml (1 pint) vegetable stock
300 ml (½ pint) milk
115 g (4 oz) unsalted peanuts
salt and freshly ground black pepper

SERVES 4–6
PREPARATION TIME: 20 minutes + overnight soaking of beans
COOKING TIME: 1 hour 40 minutes
FREEZING: recommended

HEARTY TURKEY SOUP

I first made this soup after Christmas with **leftover turkey**. However, it is so good that nowadays I also make it with cooked chicken instead of turkey – it's a really satisfying chunky main course soup. For a quicker version use 400 g/14 oz canned haricot beans instead of the dried beans.

**80 g (3 oz) dried haricot beans, soaked
   overnight in cold water**
1 tablespoon sunflower oil
1 large onion, chopped
3 celery sticks, chopped
450 g (1 lb) potatoes, diced
**675 g (1½ lb) mixed root vegetables such as
   carrot, parsnip, swede or turnip, diced**
1.1 litres (2 pints) chicken or turkey stock
225 g (8 oz) cooked turkey, shredded
salt and freshly ground black pepper

1 Drain the haricot beans, and rinse them thoroughly in cold water. Place the beans in a pan and cover with water, bring to the boil and simmer for 1 hour. Drain.
2 Place the oil in a large pan and cook the onion until soft.
3 Stir in the celery, potatoes and root vegetables and cook for 5 minutes.
4 Add the stock, haricot beans and seasoning, bring to the boil and simmer for 25 minutes or until the vegetables are soft.
5 Stir in the shredded turkey and heat through for 5 minutes. Season to taste before serving.

SERVES 4
PREPARATION TIME: 15 minutes
COOKING TIME: 12 minutes
FREEZING: not recommended

This salad can be served at any time of year – it makes a good winter salad served with cold meats and baked potatoes. But it is particularly good when made in the summer with deliciously sweet home-grown beetroot.

175 g (6 oz) pasta shapes such as farfalle or fusilli
1 tablespoon vegetable oil

FOR THE SALAD:
350 g (12 oz) cooked beetroot, diced
3 celery sticks, chopped
2 Comice pears cored, diced and coated in lemon juice
115 g (4 oz) seedless green grapes, halved
5 cm (2-inch) piece of fresh root ginger, grated finely
50 g (2 oz) Brazil nuts, chopped coarsely
2 tablespoons sunflower seeds

FOR THE DRESSING:
150 ml (¼ pint) natural yogurt
2 tablespoons soured cream
2 tablespoons lemon juice
3 tablespoons horseradish sauce
salt and freshly ground black pepper
chopped fresh mint leaves, to garnish

1 Add the pasta and vegetable oil to a large saucepan of boiling, salted water and cook according to the packet instructions. Rinse under running cold water and drain well. Allow to cool completely.
2 In a large bowl stir together the beetroot, celery, pears, grapes, root ginger, nuts and seeds. Gradually add the cooked pasta stirring well.
3 Make the dressing: in a bowl mix together the yogurt, cream, lemon juice, horseradish sauce and seasoning.
4 Stir the dressing into the salad just before serving and sprinkle with chopped mint.

BEETROOT & GINGER PASTA SALAD

SERVES 4–6
PREPARATION TIME: 20 minutes
COOKING TIME: 15 minutes
FREEZING: not recommended

The creamy cheese dressing gives this salad a refreshing tangy flavour. Replace the bulgar wheat with couscous if preferred.

115 g (4 oz) bulgar wheat
1 small Iceberg lettuce, shredded
2 small courgettes, sliced thinly
1 small onion or 3–4 spring onions, chopped finely
4 tablespoons finely chopped fresh parsley

FOR THE DRESSING:
50 g (2 oz) blue Stilton, crumbled
3 tablespoons olive oil
6 tablespoons natural yogurt
salt and freshly ground black pepper

1 In a medium saucepan cover the bulgar wheat with cold water, bring to the boil and simmer for 15 minutes. Drain well and leave to cool.
2 Place the lettuce in a large salad bowl.
3 Add the courgettes, onion or spring onions, parsley and cooled bulgar wheat to the bowl.
4 To make the dressing mix the Stilton and oil together to form a smooth paste, gradually stir in the yogurt until well blended. Season to taste.
5 Pour the dressing over the salad and toss thoroughly to coat.

ICEBERG SALAD WITH STILTON DRESSING

SERVES: 6
PREPARATION TIME: 20 minutes
FREEZING: not recommended

This **patriotic salad** uses all three varieties of Cheshire cheese – red, white and blue. Combined with apples and pears it makes a colourful and tasty main course. Serve with sun-dried tomato bread to complete the meal.

175 g (6 oz) blue Cheshire cheese, diced
115 g (4 oz) seedless black grapes, quartered
115 g (4 oz) seedless green grapes, quartered
1 round lettuce, shredded coarsely
2 firm Comice pears, cored and sliced
175 g (6 oz) white Cheshire cheese, crumbled
2 red apples cored and diced
175 g (6 oz) red Cheshire cheese, grated

FOR THE DRESSING:
4 tablespoons vegetable oil
2 tablespoons apple juice
salt and freshly ground black pepper

1 Arrange the blue Cheshire cheese and black and green grapes in the base of a large salad dish.
2 Top with a layer of lettuce and arrange the pear slices on top of the lettuce.
3 Sprinkle over the white Cheshire cheese and add another layer of lettuce. Arrange the diced apple on top and sprinkle with the red Cheshire cheese.
4 Whisk all the dressing ingredients together and drizzle over the salad just before serving.

RED, WHITE & BLUE SALAD

At the end of another busy day, the last thing you feel like doing is spending ages in the kitchen. So put your feet up, pour yourself a glass of wine and have a look through these easy to prepare and cook supper dishes. Next time you're in a rush you'll be prepared and able to get a delicious meal ready with no hassle. Rice, pasta and stir-

FAST SUPPERS

fry dishes, all of which are speedy to prepare, are included here and many of them are sure to become favourites with your family. What's more many of these recipes can be made with store cupboard ingredients, so you won't even have to step into a shop!

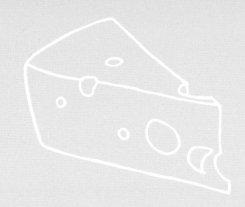

SERVES 3–4
PREPARATION TIME: 20 minutes
COOKING TIME: 15 minutes
FREEZING: not recommended

A **classic family favourite** this ever-popular dish is always a hit with children and adults alike. Serve simply with a green salad.

MACARONI CHEESE

225 g (8 oz) quick-cook dried macaroni

FOR THE CHEESE SAUCE:
40 g (1½ oz) butter
40 g (1½ oz) plain flour
575 ml (1 pint) milk
175 g (6 oz) Cheddar cheese, grated
50 g (2 oz) wholemeal breadcrumbs
salt, cayenne pepper and mustard powder,
to season

1. In a large saucepan, cook the macaroni in boiling, salted water according to the packet instructions. Drain well.
2. Make the cheese sauce: in a medium pan melt the butter. Add the flour and cook for 1 minute, stirring continuously with a wooden spoon.
3. Remove the pan from the heat and stir in the milk gradually.
4. Return the pan to the heat and bring to the boil, stirring continuously to avoid lumps. Cook the sauce for 1 minute, still stirring continuously. Remove from the heat and add salt, cayenne pepper and mustard powder to season. Add half the cheese and stir until it has melted.
5. Mix the macaroni and cheese sauce together and then place in a 1.7-litre (3-pint) pie dish.
6. Mix together the remaining cheese and breadcrumbs and sprinkle evenly over the top of the dish.
7. Brown under a preheated grill until golden brown and serve immediately.

SERVES 4
PREPARATION TIME: 20 minutes
COOKING TIME: 12 minutes
FREEZING: not recommended

This dish can be made with any leftover meat — beef, pork or lamb work equally well. Serve with steamed or boiled white rice as an accompaniment.

3 tablespoons sesame oil
I garlic clove, crushed
115 g (4 oz) spring onions, cut into matchstick pieces
3 celery sticks, sliced
I small yellow pepper, halved, de-seeded and sliced
225 g (8 oz) cucumber, cut into matchstick pieces
225 g (8 oz) beansprouts
225 g (8 oz) cooked turkey, shredded finely
225 g (8 oz) cooked smoked ham, shredded finely
30 ml (2 tablespoons) red wine vinegar
30 ml (2 tablespoons) dark soy sauce

I   In a wok or deep frying pan heat the oil over a high heat, add the garlic and cook for I minute.
2   Stir in the spring onions, celery and pepper and cook for 3–4 minutes. Add the cucumber and beansprouts and cook for 3 minutes.
3   Add the turkey and ham, and cook for 4 minutes.
4   Stir in the vinegar and soy sauce, blend well and heat until bubbling. Serve immediately.

TURKEY & HAM STIR-FRY

SERVES 4
PREPARATION TIME: 20 minutes
COOKING TIME: 8–10 minutes
FREEZING: not recommended

A tasty combination of crunchy stir-fried vegetables in a spicy peanut sauce makes a satisfying vegetarian main course. The golden rule for successful stir-frying is to ensure the vegetables are cut into pieces of approximately the same size, to ensure quick and even cooking.

80 g (3 oz) green beans, topped, tailed and cut into 5 cm (2-inch) pieces
115 g (4 oz) broccoli, sliced diagonally
2 tablespoons vegetable oil
2 garlic cloves, sliced
4 thin slices fresh root ginger
1 red chilli, de-seeded and sliced finely
115 g (4 oz) mangetout, topped and tailed
2 sticks celery, sliced diagonally
50 g (2 oz) courgettes cut into strips
150 ml (¼ pint) vegetable stock
4 tablespoons smooth peanut butter
50 g (2 oz) roasted salted peanuts
salt and freshly ground black pepper

1   Blanch the beans and broccoli in boiling, salted water for 30 seconds. Drain and refresh in cold water, drain again.
2   Heat the oil in a preheated wok or large frying pan, add the garlic, ginger and chilli and stir-fry to release the flavours.
3   Reduce the heat and add the mangetout to the pan, stir-fry for 1 minute. Add the celery, courgettes, broccoli and beans to the pan, and stir-fry for another minute until the vegetables are cooked but still crisp and bright green.
4   Stir in the vegetable stock and peanut butter, and heat through until bubbling. Add seasoning and the peanuts, and simmer for 2 minutes. Transfer to a serving dish and serve immediately.

CRUNCHY VEGETABLE SATAY STIR-FRY

MAKES 6–8
PREPARATION & COOKING TIME:
25 minutes
FREEZING: recommended

Lamb and apple plus **classic Middle Eastern flavours** of chilli and cumin combine to make these really special burgers. Cook them on the barbecue in the summer and serve in buns with salad leaves and tomato slices to garnish. Or grill them and serve with potato wedges and a spicy tomato relish.

450 g (1 lb) lean lamb mince
1 small onion, grated
1 small eating apple, grated
1 teaspoon ground cumin
1 chilli, de-seeded and chopped finely
1 egg, beaten
50 g (2 oz) fresh wholemeal breadcrumbs
1 tablespoon sunflower oil
salt and freshly ground black pepper

1 Place the lamb in a mixing bowl and add the onion, apple, cumin, chilli, egg, breadcrumbs and seasoning. Mix thoroughly.
2 Shape the mixture into 6–8 even-sized burgers.
3 Brush both sides of the burgers with the oil and cook on a preheated grill or barbecue for 5–7 minutes, on each side, until cooked right through.

LAMB & APPLE BURGERS

Pasta and chicken breasts cook quickly and take very little preparation or cooking and are ideal ingredients for a wide variety of quick supper dishes. Here they are combined with sesame seeds, ginger and coriander for a subtle Thai flavour.

SERVES 4
PREPARATION TIME: 15–20 minutes
COOKING TIME: 12–15 minutes
FREEZING: not recommended

PASTA WITH CHICKEN & CORIANDER

225 g (8 oz) dried pasta spirals
3 tablespoons sesame seeds
4 tablespoons olive oil
350 g (12 oz) skinless chicken breast, sliced
5 cm (2-inch) piece of fresh root ginger, diced finely
350 g (12 oz) leeks, cleaned and sliced thinly
3 tablespoons chopped fresh coriander
salt and freshly ground black pepper
fresh coriander leaves, to garnish

1 Bring a large saucepan of lightly salted water to the boil and cook the pasta spirals according to the packet instructions, until just tender. Drain the pasta.

2 In a small pan carefully dry fry the sesame seeds until just coloured, take care not to burn them.

3 Heat the olive oil in a deep frying pan or wok, add the chicken and diced root ginger and cook for 5 minutes. Add the sliced leeks and cook for another minute. Cover the pan and continue cooking for a further 3–5 minutes until the chicken is cooked through.

4 Stir the drained pasta into the pan or wok with the chopped coriander and sesame seeds.

5 Season to taste, toss well and serve hot, garnished with coriander leaves.

A variation on the classic Bolognese sauce – a pork, tomato and mushroom sauce is served with pasta shapes and topped with cheese. Serve with a tomato and basil salad, and a glass or two of full-bodied red wine.

SERVES 4
PREPARATION TIME: 20 minutes
COOKING TIME: 40 minutes
FREEZING: not recommended

PORK & MUSHROOM PASTA

2 tablespoons olive oil
I onion, sliced
2 carrots, sliced thinly
450 g (I lb) minced pork
225 g (8 oz) button mushrooms, quartered
150 ml (¼ pint) vegetable or chicken stock
400 g can of chopped tomatoes
I tablespoon mixed dried herbs
I tablespoon Worcestershire sauce
I tablespoon tomato purée
175 g (6 oz) dried pasta shapes
such as penne or rigatoni
salt and freshly ground black pepper
50 g (2 oz) Cheddar cheese, grated, to serve

1　Heat the oil in a large, deep frying pan and cook the onion and carrots for 5 minutes, until softened. Add the pork and cook over a medium heat until the meat has browned, stirring and breaking up with a wooden spoon, as necessary.

2　Add the mushrooms and cook for 2–3 minutes. Pour in the stock, add the tomatoes, herbs, Worcestershire sauce and tomato purée and bring to the boil.

3　Lower the heat, cover the pan and simmer gently for 30 minutes.

4　While the meat is cooking, cook the pasta in salted, boiling water for 10–12 minutes until just tender. Drain and rinse in cold water to prevent it from sticking.

5　Stir the pasta into the mince mixture and season with salt and pepper. Reheat, stirring, until bubbling. Serve topped with grated cheese.

SERVES 4
PREPARATION TIME: 15 minutes
COOKING TIME: 20 minutes
FREEZING: not recommended

STUFFED MUSHROOMS

Filled with a nutty, vegetable stuffing these mushrooms make a **healthy quick supper**. Serve with warm bread and steamed green vegetables of your choice such as mangetout, broccoli or fine beans.

4 large, flat mushrooms
15 g (½ oz) butter
1 garlic clove, crushed
3 celery sticks, chopped
50 g (2 oz) walnuts, chopped coarsely
50 g (2 oz) wholemeal breadcrumbs
1 tablespoon chopped fresh parsley
50 g (2 oz) Cheddar cheese, grated
salt and freshly ground black pepper

1   Carefully remove the stalks from the mushrooms and finely chop them.
2   In a small pan melt the butter and gently cook the chopped stalks, garlic and celery together for 5 minutes.
3   Stir in the walnuts, breadcrumbs and parsley and mix thoroughly. Season well.
4   Arrange the mushroom caps upturned on a roasting tray. Fill with the stuffing mixture and sprinkle evenly with the cheese.
5   Bake at Gas mark 6/electric oven 200°C/fan oven 180°C for 10–15 minutes until the mushrooms are tender and the cheese has turned golden brown.
6   Serve immediately.

  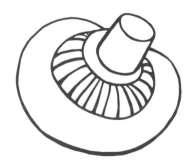

SERVES 4
PREPARATION TIME: 15 minutes
COOKING TIME: 15 minutes
FREEZING: not recommended

TUNA TAGLIATELLE

Tagliatelle served with a **hearty tuna** and tomato sauce makes a filling main course. Rocket leaves drizzled with balsamic vinegar and a little extra virgin olive oil make a delicious accompaniment.

350 g (12 oz) dried tagliatelle
200 g (7 oz) canned tuna in brine
1 tablespoon sunflower oil
2 canned anchovies, drained
and chopped finely
2 garlic cloves, chopped finely
1 red chilli, de-seeded and chopped finely
115 g (4 oz) chestnut mushrooms, sliced
225 g can of chopped tomatoes
1 tablespoon tomato purée
50 g (2 oz) stoned black olives
salt and freshly ground black pepper
chopped fresh parsley, to garnish

1   Cook the tagliatelle in a large pan of boiling, salted water according to the packet instructions until just tender. Drain the pasta.
2   Meanwhile, drain the tuna, and then flake it into chunks.
3   Heat the oil in a frying-pan; add the anchovies, garlic and chilli and fry quickly for 1 minute.
4   Stir in the mushrooms, tomatoes and tomato purée.
5   Mix well, cook gently for about 5 minutes until the mushrooms are tender.
6   Stir in the tuna, olives and seasoning and warm through.
7   Pour the tuna sauce on top of the pasta, garnish with parsley and serve.

SERVES 4
PREPARATION TIME: 20 minutes
COOKING TIME: 40 minutes
FREEZING: not recommended

Courgettes filled with a meat stuffing and beef tomatoes filled with a rice stuffing make a wonderfully colourful meal that is full of **Mediterranean flavours**. Serve with a mixed herb leaf salad and ciabatta bread.

2 large courgettes
2 tablespoons olive oil
2 large beef tomatoes

FOR THE MEAT FILLING:
175 g (6 oz) lamb mince
1 garlic clove, crushed
½ teaspoon ground coriander
2 tablespoons tomato purée
25 g (1 oz) pine kernels
50 g (2 oz) cooked brown rice
1 tablespoon chopped fresh mixed herbs
salt and freshly ground black pepper

FOR THE RICE FILLING:
50 g (2 oz) risotto rice
150 ml (¼ pint) vegetable stock
25 g (1 oz) fresh Parmesan cheese, grated
½ yellow pepper, de-seeded and chopped finely
50 g (2 oz) sun-dried tomatoes, chopped
1 teaspoon chopped fresh parsley

1   Slice the courgettes lengthways, carefully scoop out the flesh. Finely dice the flesh and brush the hollowed out shells with half the oil.
2   Slice the tops off the tomatoes and scoop out the seeds with a teaspoon. Chop the flesh from the tomato tops. Brush the tomatoes with the remaining oil.
3   To prepare the meat filling for the courgettes: dry-fry the mince until it is evenly browned. Stir in the chopped courgette flesh, crushed garlic, coriander and tomato purée. Simmer, covered for 5 minutes.
4   Add the pine kernels, chopped tomato flesh from the tomato tops, rice, mixed herbs and seasoning. Use to fill the courgette shells, packing in tightly.
5   To prepare the rice filling: place the rice in a pan with the stock, cover and simmer gently for 10–15 minutes or until the rice is tender.
6   Stir in the grated Parmesan, yellow pepper, sun-dried tomatoes, parsley and seasoning.
7   Use to fill the tomato shells.
8   Place the filled shells on a baking sheet and bake at Gas Mark 6/electric oven 200°C/fan oven 180°C for 20–25 minutes or until the courgette and tomato shells are tender.

STUFFED VEGETABLES

A **classic Italian dish** of short grain risotto rice cooked in stock with vegetables and meat. Risotto rice has a wonderfully rich and creamy texture quite unlike long-grain rice.

RISOTTO WITH SALAMI & VEGETABLES

3 tablespoons olive oil
2 red onions, sliced
1 green pepper, de-seeded and chopped
1 red pepper, de-seeded and chopped
115 g (4 oz) button mushrooms, halved
4 tomatoes, skinned and chopped
225 g (8 oz) risotto rice
850 ml (1½ pints) hot vegetable stock
225 g (8 oz) salami, cubed
salt and freshly ground black pepper
grated Parmesan cheese, to serve

1   In a deep frying pan heat the oil, add the onions and cook for 3–4 minutes. Add the peppers, mushrooms and tomatoes, stir well and cook for 3 minutes

2   Add the rice and stir to coat. Add a ladleful of hot stock and stir constantly until it is absorbed. Continue cooking in this way, adding a little hot stock at a time and stirring well between each addition. This will take 20–25 minutes.

3   Add the salami with the last ladleful of stock and stir well. The rice should be tender and creamy.

4   Season to taste and sprinkle with Parmesan cheese to serve.

Weekends are often very busy but that doesn't mean you have to compromise on what you eat. Quick and easy meals are the key to avoiding spending too much time in the kitchen. Buy good quality ingredients that require very little preparation and you're well on the way to making life easier. So whether you want a fast

SIMPLE WEEKEND LUNCHES

family meal or a more relaxed lunch for friends there are plenty of inspiring recipes to choose from here. In this chapter you will find a mixture of hearty, traditional fare and lighter dishes which take their inspiration from the Continent.

SERVES 4
PREPARATION TIME: 10 minutes
COOKING TIME: 25–30 minutes
FREEZING: not recommended

THREE CHEESE SOUFFLÉ

Soufflés always have an **air of mystery** about them. But in fact they are really easy to make — the important part is to make sure you serve them straight from the oven before they have a chance to sink. This version uses three cheeses to produce a deliciously intense flavour.

50 g (2 oz) butter
50 g (2 oz) plain flour
300 ml (½ pint) milk
5 eggs, separated
50 g (2 oz) Gruyère cheese, grated
25 g (1 oz) Parmesan, grated
50 g (2 oz) Emmenthal, grated
salt, cayenne pepper and mustard powder, to season

1 Melt the butter in a pan, stir in the flour and cook for 1 minute. Remove from the heat and gradually stir in the milk.
3 Return to the heat and bring to the boil stirring continuously until a smooth sauce is formed. Season with salt, cayenne pepper and mustard powder.
4 Cool the sauce slightly and beat in the egg yolks and cheeses.
5 In a grease-free bowl whisk the egg whites until stiff and fold into the sauce mix.
6 Pour the mixture into a well-buttered 1.1-litre (2-pint) soufflé dish.
7 Bake at Gas Mark 5/electric oven 190°C/fan oven 170°C for 25–30 minutes until golden and well risen. Serve immediately.

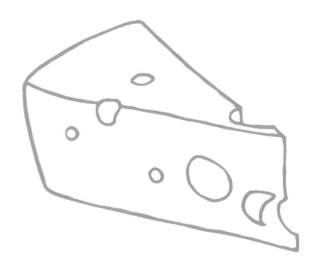

SERVES 4
PREPARATION TIME: 20 minutes
COOKING TIME: 40–50 minutes
FREEZING: recommended

SAUSAGES & KIDNEYS IN RED WINE & MUSHROOM SAUCE

A really meaty treat! Sausages and kidneys are gently cooked and then simmered in a mixture of red wine and stock. Serve with creamy mashed potatoes and stir-fried cabbage or greens.

8 lamb's kidneys
25 g (1 oz) seasoned flour
450 g (1 lb) sausages
2 tablespoons vegetable oil
8 button onions, peeled
150 ml (¼ pint) beef stock
150 ml (¼ pint) red wine
2 tablespoons tomato purée
4 bay leaves
salt and freshly ground black pepper

1. Skin the kidneys and cut them in half. Snip out the central white core with scissors and then toss them in the seasoned flour.
2. Separate the sausages and cut them in half.
3. Heat the oil in a frying-pan and gently fry the onions until pale golden.
4. Add the kidneys and sausages and fry until browned on all surfaces.
5. Stir in the stock, red wine, tomato purée and bay leaves. Bring to the boil and then reduce to a simmer. Cover and cook over a gentle heat for 40–50 minutes or until the sausages and kidneys are cooked.
6. Check the seasoning and serve immediately.

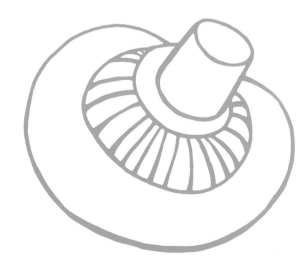

SERVES 4
PREPARATION TIME: 15 minutes
COOKING TIME: 25 minutes
FREEZING: not recommended

Brioches rolls make an unusual and **attractive shell** for this rich mushroom filling. Any combination of mushrooms can be used – look out for packets of mixed exotic mushrooms in supermarkets. Serve the brioches straight from the oven with potato wedges and salad leaves.

2 tablespoons olive oil
1 red onion, sliced
1 red pepper, de-seeded and diced
1 garlic clove, crushed
175 g (6 oz) brown chestnut mushrooms, sliced
115 g (4 oz) button mushrooms, halved
50 g (2 oz) shiitake mushrooms
150 ml (¼ pint) red wine
150 ml (¼ pint) vegetable stock
2 tablespoons cranberry sauce
4 brioches rolls
salt and freshly ground black pepper

1   Heat half the oil in a frying-pan and cook the onion, red pepper and garlic over a gentle heat until soft and cooked.
2   Add the remaining oil to the pan and gently fry the mushrooms until soft and browned.
3   Stir in the red wine, stock, cranberry sauce and seasoning and simmer for 10–15 minutes until reduced to a thick syrup.
4   While the sauce is reducing, slice the tops from the brioche rolls and using a spoon scoop out the bread from inside. Bake them at Gas Mark 6/electric oven 200°C/fan oven 180°C for 5 minutes to crisp the shells.
5   Spoon the mushroom mixture into the brioches shells and serve immediately.

MUSHROOM BRIOCHES

SERVES 4
PREPARATION TIME: 15 minutes
COOKING TIME: 35 minutes
FREEZING: not recommended

The delicate flavour of this fish is really enhanced by baking it in a delicious wine and mushroom sauce. This is a lovely dish to serve with fluffy mash potatoes and broccoli.

PLAICE WITH A WHITE WINE SAUCE

4 fillets of plaice, weighing 225 g–350 g (8 oz–12 oz) each, cleaned
175 g (6 oz) button mushrooms, cleaned and halved
425 ml (15 fl oz) white wine
25 g (1 oz) butter
25 g (1 oz) plain flour
salt and freshly ground black pepper

1   Place the fish fillets, skin side down, in a large ovenproof dish. Add the mushrooms and seasoning and pour over the wine.

2   Preheat the oven to Gas Mark 4/electric oven 180°C/fan oven 160°C. Cover the dish with a lid or foil.

3   Bake for 20–25 minutes until the fish is cooked through. To test carefully place a knife into the flesh of the fish, the flesh should be white and flaky.

4   Remove from the oven and drain the cooking juices into a jug, and keep the fish and mushrooms warm.

5   Melt the butter in a medium saucepan over a gently heat. Stir in the flour and cook for 2 minutes.

6   Gradually stir in 300 ml (1/2 pint) of the reserved cooking liquid stirring continuously to avoid lumps forming and then bring to the boil. Stir until thickened. Check the seasoning.

7   Place the fish fillets and mushrooms on serving plates and pour over the sauce. Serve immediately.

SERVES 4
PREPARATION TIME: 15 minutes
COOKING TIME: 30–35 minutes
FREEZING: not recommended

Stuffed with tomatoes, spring onions, celery and almonds then wrapped in foil and baked until tender, this simple dish takes very little effort but looks and tastes wonderful. Serve to friends with buttered new potatoes and roasted vegetables as an alternative to a Sunday roast in spring or summer.

STUFFED LAYERED TROUT

4 rainbow trout, each weighing 300–350 g (11–12 oz) cleaned
4 firm tomatoes, sliced
8 spring onions, chopped
2 celery sticks, chopped
50 g (2 oz) wholemeal breadcrumbs
50 g (2 oz) flaked almonds
2 tablespoons finely chopped fresh parsley
4 tablespoons lemon juice

1 Wash the trout and dry with kitchen paper.
2 Place slices of tomatoes in the pocket of the fish.
3 In a small bowl place the spring onions, celery, breadcrumbs, almonds and parsley, mix well and divide the mixture into four and fill the fish pockets with the stuffing.

4 Place each trout into a piece of buttered foil and sprinkle over the lemon juice and then seal.
5 Place in a baking dish and cook at Gas Mark 4/electric oven 180°C/fan oven 160°C for 30–35 minutes until the fish is cooked and tender.

SERVES 4
PREPARATION TIME: 5 minutes
COOKING TIME: 40 minutes
FREEZING: not recommended

A **classic Spanish dish** – a chunky omelette with potatoes and onions which makes a satisfying weekend lunch. Serve cut into wedges with a quick salad made from halved cherry tomatoes and chunks of cucumber.

1 tablespoon olive oil
350 g (12 oz) potatoes, sliced thinly
1 large Spanish onion, sliced thinly
6 large eggs
salt and freshly ground black pepper

1 Heat the olive oil in a large sauté pan, add the potatoes and onion and cook gently for 20–30 minutes until softened, without browning the onion.
2 Beat the eggs in large bowl, season well and add the potatoes and onion, mix thoroughly then tip back into the pan.
3 Cook over a gentle heat for 10–12 minutes until set. Place under a hot grill until golden brown.

SPANISH POTATO TORTILLA

SERVES 4
PREPARATION TIME: 20 minutes
COOKING TIME: 15 minutes
FREEZING: recommended

LIVER WITH VERMOUTH

A **tangy** one-pan liver dish flavoured with orange, lemon and vermouth. Serve with brown rice or wholemeal noodles for a tasty lunch.

450 g (1 lb) lamb's liver, sliced
1 tablespoon wholemeal flour
2 tablespoons vegetable oil
1 onion, chopped
1 garlic clove, crushed
finely grated zest and juice of 1 orange
finely grated zest and juice of 1 lemon
60 ml (4 tablespoons) sweet vermouth
2 tablespoons chopped fresh parsley
salt and freshly ground black pepper
orange and lemon slices, to garnish

1 Cut the liver into thin strips and coat in the flour.
2 Heat the oil in a flameproof casserole, add the onion and garlic to the casserole and fry gently for 5 minutes until soft but not coloured.
3 Add the liver strips and cook over a high heat until browned on all sides.
4 Add the orange and lemon zest and juices and the vermouth and bring to the boil. Stir constantly with a wooden spoon to scrape up any sediment and juices from the base of the casserole, and continue boiling until the sauce reduces.
5 Lower the heat and cook for 10 minutes or until the liver is cooked. Add half the parsley and season to taste.
6 Garnish the liver with the remaining parsley and the orange and lemon slices. Serve immediately.

SERVES 4
PREPARATION TIME: 10 minutes + 1 hour marinating
COOKING TIME: 50–60 minutes
FREEZING: not recommended

CHICKEN WITH A CITRUS SAUCE & ROASTED VEGETABLES

The citrus flavours give a modern twist to chicken to produce a great lunchtime dish; served with roasted Mediterranean vegetables it is **ideal for family meals or entertaining**. You can serve the roasted vegetables as a dish on its own or with other main courses.

4 chicken portions
grated zest and juice of 1 lemon
grated zest and juice of 1 lime
2 tablespoons olive oil
1 garlic clove, crushed
3 tablespoons orange marmalade
1 teaspoon dried mixed herbs
1 tablespoon chopped fresh parsley

FOR THE ROASTED VEGETABLES:
1 medium aubergine, sliced thickly
2 small courgettes, topped, tailed and halved lengthways
1 red pepper, quartered and de-seeded
1 yellow pepper, quartered and de-seeded
2 small red onions, quartered
4 garlic cloves, unpeeled
3 tablespoons olive oil
2 tablespoons chopped fresh thyme
115 g (4 oz) cherry tomatoes
salt and ground black pepper

1 Place the chicken portions in a shallow ovenproof dish.
2 In a small jug mix together the remaining ingredients for the chicken.
3 Pour the mixture over the chicken portions, cover and leave to marinate for 1 hour, basting occasionally.
4 Uncover and bake at Gas Mark 6/electric oven 200°C/fan oven 180°C for 50–60 minutes until crispy, golden and cooked through.
5 For the roasted vegetables, place the aubergine, courgettes, peppers, onions and garlic in a roasting tin.
6 Drizzle the olive oil over the vegetables, sprinkle the thyme over and season well.
7 Place the tin in the oven 15 minutes into the chicken's cooking time.
8 After 30 minutes. add the tomatoes and cook for a further 10–15 minutes, until the vegetables are charred and tinged brown. Serve with the chicken.

There are so many different spices available nowadays that the choice at the supermarket can be quite daunting! This chapter features a wide variety of spices ranging from versatile chilli powder to fragrant cardamom. If you're trying a spice for the first time, use it sparingly and see if you like its taste, then increase the amount

SOMETHING SPICY

used until you reach the desired flavour. Whether you're a meat-eater or vegetarian, this chapter has something for you – so stock up on a few new spices and enjoy the wonderful experience of sampling some exotic flavours.

SERVES 4–6
PREPARATION TIME: 20–25 minutes
COOKING TIME: 30–40 minutes
FREEZING: not recommended

Greek Halloumi cheese is a creamy-tasting chewy textured cheese that is most often served cooked. Here it is used to top differently coloured stuffed peppers for a light lunch. The peppers are stuffed with a spicy nut mixture flavoured with cayenne pepper. Cayenne is a pungent red, fiery-hot powder ground from the dried seeds and pods of red chillies.

ROAST HALLOUMI CHEESE PEPPERS

**6 small peppers, halved through the
stalks and deseeded
4 tablespoons olive oil
3 garlic cloves, crushed
16 fresh mint leaves, torn up
zest and juice of I lemon
3 tablespoons pine kernels
3 tablespoons flaked almonds
I tablespoon cayenne pepper
225 g (8 oz) Halloumi cheese, sliced thinly
salt and freshly ground black pepper**

1   Brush the inside and outside of the peppers with half the olive oil.
2   Place the peppers skin side down on a large baking tray.
3   In a small bowl mix together the remaining olive oil, garlic, mint leaves, lemon zest and juice, pine kernels, almonds, cayenne and seasoning. Divide this between the peppers.

4   Scatter the cheese over the top of the peppers.
5   Bake at Gas Mark 6/electric oven 200°C/fan oven 180°C for 30–40 minutes, until the peppers are tender and charred at the edges.

MAKES 6 kebabs
PREPARATION TIME: 30 minutes
+ 1 hour chilling
COOKING TIME: 15–20 minutes
FREEZING: not recommended

Each type of meat in this **colourful dish** has its own special flavouring ingredient – the lamb is enhanced with crushed garlic cloves; the minced pork is combined with coriander seeds and the steak is flavoured with horseradish sauce. Serve with dips such as tzatziki with the lamb, tomato salsa with the steak and pesto dip with the pork, and a selection of salads for easy summer entertaining.

350 g (12 oz) lean lamb, minced
350 g (12 oz) lean pork, minced
350 g (12 oz) lean steak, minced
1 large onion, grated
3 garlic cloves, crushed
1 tablespoon coriander seeds, crushed
3 tablespoons horseradish sauce
9 tablespoons finely chopped fresh mint
9 tablespoons sesame seeds, toasted
6 tablespoons poppy seeds
salt and freshly ground black pepper

1 Place each of the minced meats into a separate bowl, divide the grated onion between each and season well.
2 To the minced lamb add the crushed garlic cloves; to the minced pork add the coriander seeds; to the minced steak add the horseradish sauce.
3 Mix each of the meats thoroughly working in the flavourings.
4 Divide each mixture into eight evenly sized small balls.
5 Roll the lamb balls in the mint; the pork balls in the sesame seeds and the steak balls in the poppy seeds. Make sure each ball is evenly covered.
6 Thread four of each type of meatball on to six thin skewers and chill in the fridge for 1 hour.
7 Cook the kebabs under a hot grill: cook the pork kebabs for 12–15 minutes; the lamb kebabs for 10–12 minutes and the steak kebabs for 10 minutes, turning the skewers frequently during cooking.

SPICY KEBABS

The blend of **hot and fiery** chilli powder and mild and sweet paprika produces a hearty stew which has become a favourite with friends. Serve with hot garlic bread.

SERVES 4
PREPARATION TIME: 5 minutes
COOKING TIME: 40 minutes
FREEZING: recommended

SPICY MEATBALL STEW

450 g (1 lb) minced lamb
115 g (4 oz) fresh breadcrumbs
1 onion, grated
1 tablespoon paprika
1 garlic clove, crushed
1 teaspoon chilli powder
25 g (1 oz) pitted black olives,
roughly chopped
1 tablespoon chopped fresh parsley
1 egg, beaten
1 tablespoon vegetable oil
300 ml (½ pint) lamb stock
400 g can of chopped tomatoes
2 medium courgettes, chopped
4 bay leaves
salt and freshly ground black pepper

1 In a large bowl mix together the minced lamb, breadcrumbs, onion, paprika, garlic, chilli powder, olives, parsley and beaten egg. Ensure that the mixture is evenly combined.

2 Shape the mixture into 16 even-sized small balls.

3 Heat the oil in a frying-pan and gently fry the meatballs for 5–10 minutes until they are evenly browned.

4 Add the stock, chopped tomatoes, courgettes, bay leaves and seasoning to the pan.

5 Bring to the boil, then reduce the heat to a gentle simmer, cover the pan and cook for 30 minutes.

The **classic Indian fragrant spice** cardamom is combined with ready blended curry powder and ground cinnamon to make this really simple and healthy vegetarian curry. Serve it as a vegetarian main course for four with garlic and coriander naan bread or as an accompanying vegetable dish for eight.

SERVES 4
PREPARATION TIME: 20 minutes
COOKING TIME: 1 hour
FREEZING: recommended

LENTIL & VEGETABLE CURRY

2 tablespoons vegetable oil
1 onion, chopped finely
2 garlic cloves, crushed
2 tablespoons curry powder
6 cardamom pods, crushed
1/2 teaspoon ground cinnamon
2 bay leaves
115 g (4 oz) red lentils, rinsed well
175 g (6 oz) okra
1 aubergine, topped, tailed and cubed
2 carrots, sliced
1 cauliflower, divided into small florets
fresh bay leaves, to garnish

1. Heat the oil in a large pan, fry the onion and garlic until soft. Add the spices and bay leaves and cook for 1 minute.
2. Add the lentils and vegetables to the pan, cook for 5 minutes.
3. Pour in 850 ml (1 1/2 pints) water and bring to the boil. Reduce to a gentle simmer and cover and cook gently for 1 hour.
4. Garnish with the bay leaves before serving.

SERVES 4–6
PREPARATION TIME: 20 minutes + 6 hours marinating
COOKING TIME: 10 minutes
FREEZING: recommended

PORK SATAY

Spicy, creamy satay sauce is a southeast Asian recipe. Made from **peanuts and chilli** it is a delicious accompaniment to pork, chicken or beef. Serve with boiled rice to complete the meal.

675 g (1½ lb) pork tenderloin cut into 2.5 cm (1 inch) cubes
45 ml (3 tablespoons) olive oil, for frying

FOR THE MARINADE:
1 teaspoon chilli powder
1 teaspoon turmeric
1 teaspoon ground cumin
1 teaspoon ground coriander
½ teaspoon salt
3 tablespoons soy sauce
2 tablespoons olive oil

FOR THE SAUCE:
2 tablespoons olive oil
1 small onion, chopped finely
2 garlic cloves
4 tablespoons smooth peanut butter
1 teaspoon chilli powder
1 tablespoon soft light brown sugar
15 ml (1 tablespoon) lemon juice

1 Place the pork in a shallow dish. Mix together the marinade ingredients and pour over the pork. Cover and chill for at least 6 hours to marinate.
2 Make the sauce: in a small pan heat the oil then gently cook the onion and garlic until soft and lightly coloured. Add the peanut butter, chilli powder, sugar and lemon juice. Cook for 2 minutes.
3 Drain the pork from the marinade. In a frying pan or wok heat the olive oil and fry the pork until cooked through. Stir in the peanut sauce and heat through for 2 minutes. Serve immediately.

SERVES 4
PREPARATION TIME: 20 minutes + overnight marinating
COOKING TIME: 30 minutes
FREEZING: not recommended

CHICKEN KORMA

For the very best flavour the chicken is best left to marinate overnight in yogurt, turmeric and garlic. The mild and creamy sauce is flavoured with a **combination of fragrant spices** such as coriander seeds, ginger and cinnamon, that are fried together to release their wonderful aroma. Serve with plain naan bread or steamed rice.

1 Score each chicken breast with a sharp knife.
2 In a large bowl mix together the yogurt, garlic and turmeric, add the chicken and coat well. Cover and marinate overnight in the fridge.
3 In a large frying pan melt the butter, add the onion and cook until soft and browned, stir in the ginger, chilli powder, coriander seeds, cloves, salt and cinnamon stick and cook for 2–3 minutes.
4 Add the chicken and its marinade and cook on a gentle heat for 20–25 minutes until the chicken is completely cooked.
5 Blend the cornflour and cream together and stir into the chicken, reheat very gently to prevent the cream from curdling.
6 Sprinkle over the cashew nuts to serve.

4 boneless, skinless chicken breasts
150 ml ($\frac{1}{4}$ pint) natural yogurt
2 garlic cloves, crushed
2 teaspoons turmeric
40 g ($1\frac{1}{2}$ oz) unsalted butter
1 large onion, sliced
5 cm (2-inch) piece of fresh root ginger, peeled and diced finely
1 teaspoon chilli powder
1 teaspoon coriander seeds, crushed
10 whole cloves
1 teaspoon salt
5 cm (2-inch) piece of cinnamon stick
1 tablespoon cornflour
150 ml ($\frac{1}{4}$ pint) single cream
25 g (1 oz) unsalted cashew nuts, to serve

SERVES 4
PREPARATION TIME: 20 minutes
COOKING TIME: 40–45 minutes
FREEZING: recommended

Many traditional Provençal dishes feature generous amounts of garlic, this chunky casserole uses just a couple of cloves, but if you prefer a stronger flavour add a couple more. Any firm-fleshed white fish such as monkfish or haddock can replace the cod in this dish.

2–3 tablespoons olive oil
2 large onions, chopped roughly
2 garlic cloves, chopped roughly
2 tablespoons coarsely chopped fresh parsley
450 g (1 lb) tomatoes, skinned and chopped roughly
115 ml (4 fl oz) dry white wine
1 teaspoon fresh or ½ teaspoon dried marjoram
4 cod steaks (approx 675 g/1½ lb total weight), skinned
50 g (2 oz) black olives
1 tablespoon tomato purée
salt and freshly ground black pepper
fresh parsley, to garnish

1   Heat the oil in a large deep frying pan and gently fry the onions, garlic and parsley over a low heat for 5–8 minutes.
2   Add the tomatoes. Mix well, and then stir in the wine, marjoram and seasoning.
3   Simmer, uncovered, for about 20 minutes.
4   Place the cod steaks in the pan and cover with the sauce. Add the olives and stir in the tomato purée. Cook, uncovered, over a very gentle heat for 20–25 minutes.
5   Serve garnished with fresh parsley.

PROVENÇAL FISH CASSEROLE

SERVES 4
PREPARATION TIME: 20 minutes
COOKING TIME: 1½–2 hours
FREEZING: recommended

BEEF OLIVES

A time-honoured dish of slices of beef rolled around a simple vegetable stuffing. They look really impressive, but are quick and easy to prepare.

450 g (1 lb) topside of beef
2 medium carrots, diced finely
1 large onion, diced finely
1 teaspoon dried mixed herbs
2 tablespoons tomato purée
1 tablespoon Worcestershire sauce
2 teaspoons cornflour blended with a little cold water
300 ml (½ pint) beef stock
salt and freshly ground black pepper
1 tablespoon finely chopped fresh parsley, to garnish

1   Slice the topside into four thick slices. Place each slice between greaseproof paper and flatten it by bashing it with a rolling pin.
2   Sprinkle the slices with salt and pepper.
3   In a bowl mix together the carrots, onion, herbs, tomato purée, Worcestershire sauce, blended cornflour and 4 tablespoons of the stock.
4   Divide the stuffing mixture between the flattened slices and roll each up into a neat parcel. Tie each parcel securely with string.
5   Place the olives in a shallow roasting dish and pour in the remaining stock. Cover the dish tightly with foil and cook at Gas Mark 4/electric oven 180°C/fan oven 160°C for 1½–2 hours or until the meat is really tender.
6   To serve, remove the string from each beef olive and garnish with parsley.

SERVES 4
PREPARATION TIME: 20 minutes
COOKING TIME: 2 hours 20 minutes
FREEZING: recommended

LANCASHIRE HOTPOT

A traditional northern dish which consists of layers of lamb, sliced onions and potatoes cooked in a pot. Boiled carrots or mashed swede are ideal accompaniments.

675 g (1½ lb) middle or best end of neck lamb chops
25 g (1 oz) plain flour
2 large onions, sliced
2 lamb's kidneys, skinned, cored and sliced
675 g (1½ lb) potatoes, sliced
25 g (1 oz) butter melted
425 ml (¾ pint) lamb stock
salt and freshly ground black pepper

1   Trim any excess fat from the chops. Mix together the flour and seasoning and coat the chops evenly in seasoned flour.
2   Arrange layers of meat, onion, kidney and potatoes in a large casserole dish. Season each layer with salt and pepper and finish with a layer of potatoes.
3   Brush the top of the potatoes with melted butter.
4   Pour the stock into the casserole dish and cover it tightly with a lid or foil.
5   Cook the hotpot at Gas Mark 4/electric oven 180°C/fan oven 160°C for 1½–2 hours, or until the meat is tender.
6   Remove the lid or foil from the casserole and cook for an extra 20 minutes to brown the potatoes.

SERVES: 4–6
PREPARATION TIME: 10 minutes + 4 hours soaking
COOKING TIME: 1–1¼ hours
FREEZING: not recommended

BOILED BACON & PEASE PUDDING

An old English dish of bacon boiled with split peas. The peas absorb the wonderful meaty flavour from the cooking liquid – an ideal winter dish. Serve with mashed potatoes and carrots.

900 g (2 lb) bacon joint
225 g (8 oz) split peas
salt and freshly ground black pepper

1   Soak the bacon joint in cold water for at least 4 hours, drain.
2   Soak the split peas in cold water for 2–3 hours, drain.
3   Place the bacon and peas in a large pan and completely cover with cold water.
4   Bring to the boil and remove any scum from the top of the water.
5   Reduce the heat to a simmer and cook for 1–1¼ hours.
6   Remove the bacon from the pan and drain the pease pudding. Season to taste before serving.

SERVES 4
PREPARATION TIME: 35 minutes
COOKING TIME: 2 hours
FREEZING: recommended

A **traditional British stew** of chunks of beef cooked in Guinness until tender, with an American twist – the meat is topped with a layer of light scones towards the end of the cooking time. Serve with a selection of green vegetables.

50 g (2 oz) plain flour
½ teaspoon grated nutmeg
675 g (1½ lb) chuck steak, cut into
2.5 cm (1-inch) cubes
3 tablespoons olive oil
25 g (1 oz) butter
2 large onions, sliced finely
2 garlic cloves, crushed
1 teaspoon brown sugar
575 ml (1 pint) Guinness
zest and juice of 1 orange
1 bay leaf
salt and freshly ground black pepper

FOR THE SCONE TOPPING:
225 g (8 oz) self-raising flour
a pinch of salt
50 g (2 oz) butter
7 tablespoons milk

1 Sift the flour into a shallow dish and stir in the nutmeg and plenty of seasoning. Coat the meat in the flour.
2 Heat half the oil and half the butter in a flameproof casserole. Add half the meat and fry for 2–3 minutes until evenly browned. Transfer to a plate, add the remaining oil and butter to the casserole and brown the remaining meat. Transfer to the plate.
3 Put the onions and garlic in the casserole and fry gently for 5 minutes, stirring constantly.
4 Add the sugar to the casserole and cook over a moderate heat for a further minute, stirring constantly, until the sugar caramelises.
5 Return the beef to the casserole and pour the Guinness over the top. Add the orange juice and zest and bay leaf and bring to the boil.
6 Cover and cook at Gas Mark 4/electric oven 180°C/fan oven 160°C for 1–1½ hours, stirring occasionally, adding a little water to the casserole if the liquid becomes too thick.
7 To make the scone topping, sift the flour and salt into a bowl and rub the butter in until the mixture forms fine breadcrumbs. Add enough milk to form a soft dough. Knead on a lightly floured surface and roll out to 1 cm (½ inch) thick and cut out 12 scones using a 5 cm (2-inch) cutter.
8 After 1½ hours cooking time remove the meat from the oven, take off the lid and arrange the scones in an overlapping circle around the edge of the dish.
9 Return the dish, uncovered, to the oven and cook for a further 30 minutes or until the scones are well-risen and golden brown.

BEEF IN GUINNESS COBBLER

SERVES 4–6
PREPARATION TIME: 20 minutes
COOKING TIME: 1 hour
FREEZING: not recommended

A minced meat layer topped with mashed potatoes was traditionally made to use up leftover meat from the Sunday roast lamb. Nowadays, however it is much more often made from raw minced lamb. Serve with steamed cabbage on a cold day.

SHEPHERD'S PIE

2 tablespoons olive oil
1 large onion, chopped
450 g (1 lb) minced lamb
115 g (4 oz) button mushrooms, sliced
400 g can of chopped tomatoes
1 teaspoon Worcestershire sauce
150 ml (¼ pint) lamb stock
675 g (1½ lb) potatoes peeled and chopped
2 tablespoons milk
15 g (½ oz) butter
salt and freshly ground black pepper

1. In a frying-pan heat the oil and fry the onion until soft.
2. Add the lamb and cook until browned. Stir in the mushrooms and cook for 3 minutes.
3. Add the tomatoes, Worcestershire sauce, stock and seasoning. Bring to the boil and then simmer gently for 25 minutes.
4. Place the potatoes and 1 teaspoon of salt in a pan, cover with cold water and bring to the boil. Reduce the heat to simmer and cook for 15 minutes or until the potatoes are soft. Drain and return the potatoes to the pan, then mash with milk and butter.
5. Place the meat in a 1-litre (1¾-pint) shallow dish and evenly spread the mashed potato over the meat. Using a fork mark a pattern in the potatoes.
6. Cook at Gas Mark 5/electric oven 190°C/fan oven 170°C for 25–30 minutes or until the potatoes are crisp and golden brown

SERVES 4
PREPARATION TIME: 20 minutes
COOKING TIME: 30 minutes
FREEZING: not recommended

Fish in a parsley sauce topped with creamy mash – a family favourite that is popular with children and grown-ups. It can be made with any white or smoked fish or a mixture of both; for an extra flavour add some grated mature Cheddar cheese to the potato. Serve with broccoli, green beans or peas.

FISHERMAN'S PIE

450 g (I lb) cod or haddock fillets, skinned
300 ml (½ pint) milk plus 2 tablespoons
675 g (I½ lb) potatoes, chopped
50 g (2 oz) butter
25 g (I oz) plain flour
I tablespoon chopped fresh parsley
salt and freshly ground black pepper

1 Remove any bones from the fish and cut it into chunks. Place in a shallow 1-litre (1¾-pint) dish, pour over the 300 ml (½ pint) milk and poach at Gas Mark 5/electric oven 190°C/fan oven 170°C for 20 minutes. Drain and reserve the poaching liquid.

2 Place the potatoes and 1 teaspoon of salt in a pan, cover with cold water and bring to the boil. Reduce the heat to simmer and cook for 15 minutes or until the potatoes are soft. Drain and return the potatoes to the pan, then mash with the 2 tablespoons of milk and half the butter.

3 To make the sauce, melt the remaining butter in a medium pan. Stir in the flour and cook for 1 minute, remove from the heat and gradually stir in the reserved poaching liquid. Return to the heat and bring to the boil stirring continuously. Remove from the heat, season and stir in the chopped parsley.

4 Stir the fish into the parsley sauce and place in a shallow 1-litre (1¾-pint) dish. Spread the mash evenly over the fish sauce and using a fork mark a pattern in the potatoes.

5 Place under a hot grill until the top is crispy and golden brown.

SERVES 4
PREPARATION TIME: 25 minutes
COOKING TIME: 40 minutes
FREEZING: recommended (sauce only)

SPAGHETTI BOLOGNESE

A classic Italian dish that is popular worldwide. This version includes white wine rather than the more commonly used red wine, to produce a light sauce which is really delicious.

15 g (½ oz) butter
50 g (2 oz) bacon, chopped
1 large onion, chopped finely
2 carrots, diced
2 celery sticks, chopped
350 g (12 oz) minced beef
3 tablespoons tomato purée
1 teaspoon dried oregano
150 ml (¼ pint) dry white wine
150 ml (¼ pint) beef stock
225 g (8 oz) dried spaghetti
salt and freshly ground black pepper
grated Parmesan cheese, to serve

1 In a deep frying-pan melt the butter, add the bacon and fry for 2–3 minutes. Add the onion, carrots and celery and fry for 5 minutes until lightly browned.
2 Add the meat to the pan and brown lightly.
3 Stir in the tomato purée, oregano, wine and stock, season and bring to the boil. Lower the heat and simmer for 30–40 minutes until the sauce is reduced and thick.
4 Cook the spaghetti in boiling, lightly salted water according to the packet instructions.
5 Drain the spaghetti and serve on a warmed serving dish topped with the meat sauce. Sprinkle with grated Parmesan cheese, to serve.

SERVES 4
PREPARATION TIME: 30 minutes
COOKING TIME: 45–50 minutes
FREEZING: recommended

PORK IN CIDER WITH HERBY DUMPLINGS

This warming casserole is served with light herby dumplings, which are cooked on the top of the dish and absorb lots of the **wonderful flavours**.

1 tablespoon olive oil
675 g (1½ lb) lean boneless pork, cubed
1 onion, sliced
2 tablespoons plain flour
1 litre (1¾ pints) dry cider
2 carrots, chopped
2 eating apples, cored and sliced
1 bouquet garni
2 tablespoons Dijon mustard
2 tablespoons Worcestershire sauce
salt and freshly ground black pepper

FOR THE HERBY DUMPLINGS:
115 g (4 oz) self-raising flour
50 g (2 oz) shredded beef or vegetable suet
2 tablespoons chopped fresh mixed herbs,
    such as parsley, sage and thyme or
    2 teaspoons dried mixed herbs

1 Heat the oil in a large saucepan and fry the pork until browned, then remove with a slotted spoon and set aside. Add the onion to the pan and fry for 5 minutes until lightly browned. Stir in the flour and cook for 1 minute, then gradually stir in the cider until smooth.

2 Return the pork to the pan with the carrots, apples, bouquet garni, Dijon mustard and Worcestershire sauce, season well. Cover and simmer for 30 minutes.

3 Meanwhile, make the herby dumplings: mix the flour, suet, herbs and seasoning together. Add 3–4 tablespoons of water and mix lightly to a soft dough. Shape into eight balls and add to the casserole, slightly apart. Cover and simmer for a further 15–20 minutes until the dumplings are risen and light.

SERVES 4–6
PREPARATION TIME: 15 minutes
+ 30 minutes for salting the aubergine
COOKING TIME: 1¼ hours
FREEZING: recommended

Layers of pasta sheets, meat sauce and cheese sauce make up this traditional Italian main course. Aubergine is included in the meat sauce in this version for an added flavour. Serve with rocket leaves drizzled with balsamic vinegar and a little extra virgin olive oil.

1 medium aubergine
25 g (1 oz) butter
1 garlic clove, crushed
350 g (12 oz) minced beef
1 teaspoon plain flour
350 g (12 oz) tomatoes, skinned and chopped
2 tablespoons tomato purée
300 ml (½ pint) dry white wine
2 teaspoons dried mixed herbs
225 g (8 oz) no pre-cook dried lasagne
salt and freshly ground black pepper

FOR THE CHEESE SAUCE:
25 g (1 oz) butter
25 g (1 oz) plain flour
300 ml (½ pint) milk
115 g (4 oz) Cheddar cheese, grated

1 Slice the aubergine and sprinkle with salt, leave for 30 minutes, pat dry.
2 Heat the butter in a large frying-pan and fry the aubergine slices and garlic together until soft.
3 Add the minced beef and fry until brown. Stir in the flour and cook for 2 minutes.
4 Add the tomatoes, tomato purée, wine and herbs, season and bring to the boil, simmer for 30 minutes.
5 Make the cheese sauce, melt the butter in a medium pan. Stir in the flour and cook for 1 minute, remove from the heat and gradually mix in the milk. Return to the heat and bring to the boil stirring continuously. Remove from the heat and stir in half the cheese.
6 Grease a large shallow ovenproof dish.
7 Arrange a layer of lasagne on the base of the dish, top with half the meat sauce, then half the cheese sauce. Repeat the layers and sprinkle with the remaining grated cheese.
8 Bake at Gas Mark 5/electric oven 190°C/fan oven 170°C for 30–40 minutes until golden brown.

LASAGNE

Entertaining friends and family should be fun and stress-free. You should be able to relax and enjoy a drink with your guests while the food looks after itself. From simple casseroles that can be prepared well in advance to baked chicken, fish, lamb or pork recipes you're bound to be inspired by many of the dishes in this chapter. And keep accompaniments simple too – there are so many delicious breads

HASSLE-FREE ENTERTAINING

available nowadays, lots of fresh salad ingredients to choose from and a wide variety of rices and grains that take very little effort to cook. Entertaining has never been so easy so keep it hassle-free and enjoy!

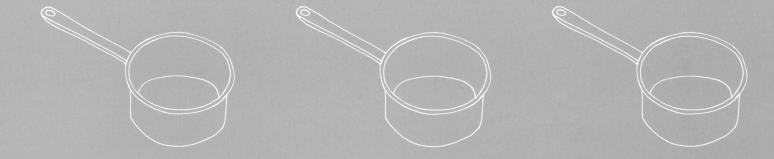

This rich and tasty dish is **lovely** made with fresh chestnuts, but can also be made with dried or canned – simply add them to the casserole in step 4. Serve the casserole with mashed potato and a selection of vegetables.

VENISON & CHESTNUT CASSEROLE

18 fresh chestnuts
3 tablespoons olive oil
3 shallots, chopped finely
4 rashers unsmoked streaky bacon, chopped
3 celery sticks, chopped
25 g (1 oz) plain flour
675 g (1½ lb) venison, diced
425 ml (¾ pint) beef stock
150 ml (¼ pint) red wine
8 juniper berries, crushed lightly
45 ml (3 tablespoons) Grand Marnier
salt and freshly ground black pepper

1 To prepare the fresh chestnuts, make a slit in each one, place in a pan of boiling water and simmer for 10 minutes. Remove a couple at a time and carefully remove the outer and inner skin. If the inner skin remains, place the chestnuts in fresh boiling water and boil for a further 3 minutes, the skin will then rub off easily.

2 Heat the oil in a large frying-pan or deep pan and fry the shallots gently until cooked.

3 Stir in the bacon and celery and cook for 3–4 minutes.

4 Mix together the flour and seasoning and coat the venison in the seasoned flour. Add to the pan and fry until browned on all surfaces.

5 Stir in the stock and wine and bring to the boil, add the chestnuts, juniper berries and Grand Marnier.

6 Place in a casserole dish, cover and cook at Gas Mark 3/electric oven 170°C/fan oven 150°C for 1½–1¾ hours or until the meat is tender.

SERVES 4
PREPARATION TIME: 20 minutes
COOKING TIME: 45–60 minutes
FREEZING: not recommended

Fresh tuna is a meaty fish and has quite a different flavour from the canned variety. This meal is cooked in one dish to combine the **great flavours** of the vegetables and fish, and only needs a simple accompaniment of crusty bread. Salmon steaks can be used as an alternative.

1 aubergine, sliced
1 onion, chopped
2 carrots, sliced thinly
2 courgettes, sliced
4 tomatoes, quartered
50 g (2 oz) butter
4 tuna steaks, approx 225–300 g
(8–11 oz) each
salt and freshly ground black pepper

FOR THE TOPPING:
115 g (4 oz) wholemeal breadcrumbs
50 g (2 oz) Cheddar cheese, grated
1 cooking apple, cored and chopped finely

1 Place the aubergine, onion, carrots, courgettes, and tomatoes into an ovenproof dish, season well.
2 Dot the vegetables with the butter, then place the tuna steaks on top of the vegetables.
3 In a small bowl combine the topping ingredients and spread evenly over the fish.
4 Bake at Gas Mark 4/electric oven 180°C/fan oven 160°C for 45–60 minutes until the vegetables and fish cooked.
5 Serve as a stack with the vegetables underneath the tuna.

TUNA STACKS

SERVES 4
PREPARATION TIME: 20 minutes
+ 1 hour marinating
COOKING TIME: 30–40 minutes
FREEZING: recommended

Chicken breasts are marinated in mustard and wine and then baked in the oven with courgettes, carrots and mushrooms. A **simple** all-in-one meal that can be prepared in advance and then cooked just before serving. Rice or baked potatoes are good with this dish.

4 boneless, skinless chicken breasts
300 ml (½ pint) white wine
4 tablespoons Dijon mustard
3 tablespoons olive oil
2 medium courgettes, topped, tailed and sliced
4 small carrots, diced
115 g (4 oz) button mushrooms
2 tablespoons cornflour
300 ml (½ pint) chicken stock

1 Cut each chicken breast into six slices and place the slices in a shallow dish.
2 Mix together the white wine and Dijon mustard and pour over the chicken. Leave to marinate, covered, in the fridge for at least 1 hour.
3 In a frying-pan heat the oil and add the chicken strips to the pan and brown on all sides. Add the courgettes, carrots and mushrooms and cook for 5 minutes.
4 Mix the cornflour with a little of the stock and add to the frying pan with the remaining stock and the marinade.
5 Heat gently until the sauce has thickened.
6 Transfer to a casserole dish, cover and cook at Gas Mark 4/electric oven 180°C/ fan oven 160°C, for 30–40 minutes until the chicken is cooked right through.

CHICKEN IN DIJON SAUCE

SERVES 4
PREPARATION TIME: 20 minutes +1 hour marinating
COOKING TIME: 50–60 minutes
FREEZING: recommended

MEDITERRANEAN LAMB

The flavours of this dish are reminiscent of Greek holidays – the lamb is marinated in a spicy yogurt mixture and then gently simmered in a tomato sauce. Serve with plain boiled rice and a green salad.

225 g (8 oz) Greek yogurt
zest of 1 lemon
2 garlic cloves, crushed
3 tablespoons olive oil
1 teaspoon ground cumin
675 g (1½ lb) tenderloin of lamb, cubed
1 onion, sliced thinly
150 ml (¼ pint) dry white wine
1 lamb stock cube, crumbled
400 g can of chopped tomatoes
1 tablespoon tomato purée
1 teaspoon caster sugar
2 bay leaves
1 tablespoon fresh oregano
80 g (3 oz) stoned black olives
175 g (6 oz) artichoke hearts
salt and freshly ground black pepper
6 mint leaves, chopped finely

1 Spoon 3 tablespoons of the Greek yogurt into a bowl and stir in the lemon zest, garlic, 1 tablespoon of the oil, seasoning and cumin. Place the lamb in the marinade and coat well. Place in the fridge for at least 1 hour to marinate.

2 Heat the remaining oil in a large frying-pan and fry the onion over a gentle heat until tender. Add the meat and fry until browned on all surfaces.

3 Pour the wine into the frying-pan and stir well. Add the stock cube, tomatoes, tomato purée, sugar, bay leaves and oregano.

4 Cover the pan and simmer very gently until the meat is tender for about 50–60 minutes.

5 Stir in the olives and artichoke hearts and cook for 10 minutes.

6 Serve with the remaining Greek yogurt mixed with the chopped mint leaves.

SERVES 4
PREPARATION TIME: 15 minutes
COOKING TIME: 30 minutes
FREEZING: recommended

MADEIRA PORK

A creamy sauce flavoured with Madeira and mushrooms – a simple but delicious dish. Ruby port can be used in place of the Madeira if you prefer. Serve with buttered noodles and your favourite green vegetable.

2–3 tablespoons sunflower oil
1 onion, chopped
1 large yellow pepper, de-seeded and diced
675 g (1½ lb) pork fillet, trimmed and cut into 1 cm (½-inch) slices
1 tablespoon paprika
1 tablespoon plain flour
300 ml (½ pint) stock
150 ml (¼ pint) Madeira
175 g (6 oz) button mushrooms
1 tablespoon tomato purée
150 ml (¼ pint) single cream
salt and freshly ground black pepper

1 Heat the oil in a large frying-pan. Add the onion and pepper to the pan and cook for 3–4 minutes.
2 Add the pork slices to the pan and brown on all sides. Stir in the paprika and flour and cook for 1 minute.
3 Blend in the stock and Madeira, bring to the boil, and reduce the heat to simmer, stir in the mushrooms, tomato purée and seasoning.
4 Cover the pan and simmer gently for 20 minutes or until the pork is tender and cooked through.
5 Stir in the cream, heat gently and serve straight away.

SERVES 4
PREPARATION TIME: 25 minutes
COOKING TIME: 25–30 minutes
FREEZING: recommended

BRAISED PORK WITH FENNEL

A simple pork casserole made with just six ingredients, but full of taste. The subtle flavour of the fennel enhances the pork and adds a sweetness to the finished dish. Serve with roasted sweet potatoes.

2 tablespoons sunflower oil
4 pork steaks, approx 175–225 g (6–8 oz) each
225 g (8 oz) fennel bulb
1 red pepper, de-seeded and diced
225 g (8 oz) mushrooms wiped and quartered
400 g can chopped tomatoes
salt and freshly ground black pepper

1 Heat the oil in a frying-pan and brown the steaks on both sides. Place in a large shallow roasting dish.
2 Thinly slice the fennel and reserve any feathery leaves for garnish.
3 Cook the fennel slices in the frying-pan until softened and place on top of the pork in the dish.
4 Fry the pepper and mushrooms until soft for about 5 minutes, stir in the tomatoes and bring to the boil. Add seasoning. Pour the sauce over the pork in the dish and cover with a lid or foil.
5 Cook at Gas Mark 6/electric oven 200°C/fan oven 180°C for 25–30 minutes until the pork is cooked through and the vegetables are tender.
6 Serve garnished with the feathery fennel leaves.

SERVES 4
PREPARATION TIME: 25 minutes
COOKING TIME: 30–40 minutes
FREEZING: recommended

Papaya, orange, ginger and caramelised onions make a **wonderful combination** of ingredients for stuffing chicken breasts. The breasts are wrapped in bacon and foil to seal in all the delicious flavours during cooking. Serve with wild and long grain rice and broccoli or sugar snap peas.

I onion, diced finely
2 tablespoons sunflower oil
I teaspoon brown sugar
5 cm (2-inch) piece of fresh root ginger, peeled and diced finely
100 g (3½ oz) dried papaya, chopped
I orange
150 ml (¼ pint) white wine
4 boneless, skinless chicken breasts
12 rashers smoked streaky bacon
salt and freshly ground black pepper

1 Place the onion and oil in a medium saucepan and cook over a gentle heat for 10 minutes, until the onion is soft. Sprinkle in the sugar, increase the heat to high and cook for 2–3 minutes until caramelised.
2 Add the ginger and papaya to the onions. Grate the zest from the orange and add to the pan. Peel the orange, chop up the flesh and add to the pan with the white wine and heat the mixture until boiling. Add seasoning.
3 Place 2 tablespoons of mixture into the pocket in each chicken breast. Reserve the remaining mixture.
4 Wrap three rashers of bacon tightly around each chicken breast to enclose the filling and wrap each breast securely in foil.
5 Place in a baking dish and cook at Gas Mark 5/electric oven 190°C/fan oven 170°C for 30–40 minutes or until the chicken is cooked through completely.
6 Purée the remaining onion and orange mixture and heat through and serve with the chicken.

GINGERED ORANGE CHICKEN

SERVES 4
PREPARATION TIME: 15 minutes
COOKING TIME: 30 minutes
FREEZING: not recommended

This tangy plum sauce goes really well with rich duck meat. Victoria plums give the most intense flavour, but other varieties are available throughout the year and enable this **simple dish** to be prepared any time. Serve with bulgar wheat or couscous.

4 duck breasts
2 tablespoons olive oil
2 shallots, chopped finely
225 g (8 oz) plums, stoned and quartered
150 ml (¼ pint) red wine
zest and juice of 1 orange
2 tablespoons clear honey
3 tablespoons cranberry sauce
15 g (½ oz) unsalted butter

1 Score the duck fat three or four times with a sharp knife. Place the duck breasts in a roasting dish and roast at Gas Mark 6/electric oven 200°C/fan oven 180°C for 20–30 minutes until cooked through.
2 In a pan heat the oil and then gently cook the shallots without colouring.
3 Stir in the plums and cook for 5 minutes.
4 Add the red wine, orange zest and juice and honey. Cook for 8–10 minutes. Allow to cool for 5 minutes.
5 Purée the sauce, then sieve it and pour it back into the pan. Heat to reduce by one-third, stir in the cranberry sauce and butter and heat through. If the sauce is too sharp adjust to taste by adding an extra spoonful of honey
6 Remove the skin from the cooked duck breasts and slice the meat. Serve with the sauce.

DUCK BREASTS WITH PLUM SAUCE